I Love You

-God

To: _____

Here is a special gift for you

From: _____

Date: _____

"*Love* is patient, *love* is kind. It does not envy, it does not boast, it is not proud. It is not rude, it is not self-seeking, it is not easily angered, it keeps no record of wrongs. *Love* does not delight in evil but rejoices with the truth. It always protects, always trusts, always hopes, always perseveres. *Love* never fails…

1 Corinthians 13:4-7

"Dear friends, let us *love* one another, for *love* comes from God. Everyone who loves has been born of God and knows God. Whoever does not *love* does not know God, because God is *love*." 1 John 4:7-8

Behold, you are beautiful, my *love*, Behold, you are beautiful; your eyes are doves.

Song of Solomon 1:15

Satisfy us in the morning with your steadfast *love*, that we may rejoice and be glad all our days.

"Be completely humble and gentle; be patient, bearing with one another in love."

Ephesians 4:2

Mercy, peace and love be yours in abundance.

Jude 1:2

Dear Children, let us not *love* with words or speech but with actions and in truth.

1 John 3:18

You, Lord, are forgiving and good, abounding in *love* to all who call to you.

Psalm 86:5

Whoever pursues righteousness and love

finds life, prosperity and honor.
Proverbs 21:21

"So now faith, hope, and *love* abide, these three; but the greatest of these is *love*."

1 Corinthians 13:13

May the Lord make your love increase and ♥ *overflow for each other…*

1 Thessalonians 3:12

"Let all that you do be done in love."

1 Corinthians 16:14

"But *love* your enemies, do good to them, and lend to them without expecting to get anything back. Then your reward will be great, and you will be sons of the Most High, for he is kind to the ungrateful and the evil. Luke 6:35

My beloved is mine, and I am his; 💙

Song of Solomon 2:16

"*Love* must be sincere. Hate what is evil; cling to what is good. Be devoted to one another in *love.* Honor one another above yourselves."

Romans 12:9-10

"No one can serve two masters. Either you will hate the one and *love* the other, or you will be devoted to the one and despise the other. You cannot serve both God and money."

Luke 16:13

And above all these put on *love*, which
binds them all together in perfect harmony. ♥

Colossians 3:14

Place me like a seal over your heart,

like a seal on your arm;

for love is as strong as death,

its jealousy unyielding as the grave.

It burns like blazing fire,

like a mighty flame. Many waters cannot quench love;

rivers cannot sweep it away. If one were to give all the

wealth of one's house for love, it would be utterly

scorned.

Song of Songs 8:6-7

"But the fruit of the Spirit is *love*..

Galatians 5:22

"Owe no one anything, except to love each other, for the one who loves another has fulfilled the law."

Romans 13:8

Love and faithfulness meet together; 💙
righteousness and peace kiss each other.
Psalm 85:10

Jesus replied: " 'Love the Lord your God with all your heart and with all your soul and with all your mind'. Matthew 22:37

"*The earth is filled with your love, Lord;…*"

Psalm 119:64

Behold, you are beautiful, my love, behold, you are beautiful!

Song of Solomon 4:1

Dear friends, since God so loved us, we also ought to *love* one another.

1 John 4:11

"Let *love* and faithfulness never leave you;
bind them around your neck, write them on
the tablet of your heart.
Proverbs 3:3

"There is no fear in *love*. But perfect *love* drives out fear, because fear has to do with punishment. The one who fears is not made perfect in *love*.

"*Because your* *Love* *is better than life, my lips will glorify you.*"

Psalm 63:3

I am my beloved's,

and his desire is for me.

Song of Solomon 7:10

My command is this: *Love* each other as I have loved you. *Greater love has no one than this: to lay down one's life for one's friends."*
John 15:12-13

Jacob was in *love* with Rachel and said, "I'll work for you seven years in return for your younger daughter Rachel." 💙

So Jacob served seven years to get Rachel, but they seemed like only a few days to him because of his *love* for her. 💙

Genesis 29:18, 20

Love the LORD your God with all your heart and with all your soul and with all your strength.
Deuteronomy 6:5

I grieve for you, Jonathan my brother; you were very dear to me. Your *love* for me was wonderful, more wonderful than that of women.

2 Samuel 1:26

See what kind of *love* the Father has given to us, that we should be called children of God;….

1 John 3:1

"Above all, *love* each other deeply, because *love* covers over a multitude of sins."

1 Peter 4:8

You are altogether beautiful, my *love*;
there is no flaw in you.
Song of Solomon 4:7

"Hatred stirs up strife, but *love* covers all offenses." 💙

Proverbs 10:12

"But you are a forgiving God, gracious and compassionate, slow to anger and abounding in love..."

Nehemiah 9:17

"Your *love,* Lord, reaches to the heavens, your faithfulness to the skies. Your righteousness is like the highest mountains, your justice like the great deep."

Psalm 36:5-6

Give thanks to the LORD, for he is good; his *love* endures forever. 💙

1 Chronicles 16:34

Behold, you are beautiful, my beloved, truly delightful.

Song of Solomon 1:16

A friend *loves* at all times,....

Proverbs 17:17

If anyone says, "I *love* God," and hates his brother, he is a liar; for he who does not *love* his brother whom he has seen cannot *love* God whom he has not seen. 1 John 4:20

"his banner over me was love."

Song of Songs 2:4

But let all who take refuge in you rejoice;
let them ever sing for joy, and spread your protection over
them, that those who *Love* your name may exult in you.

Psalm 5:11

Love the Lord your God with all your heart and with all your soul and with all your mind and with all your strength.

The second is this: '*Love* your neighbor as yourself. There is no commandment greater than these."

Mark 12:30-31

We *love* because he first loved us.

1 John 4:19

Husbands, *love* your wives, just as Christ loved the church and gave himself up for her In this same way, husbands ought to *love* their wives as their own bodies. He who loves his wife loves himself.

Ephesians 5: 25, 28

Husbands, *love* your wives and do not be harsh with them.

Colossians 3:19

honor your father and mother', and 'love your neighbor as yourself.'

Matthew 19:19

How beautiful and pleasant you are,
*O **loved** one, with all your delights!*
Song of Solomon 7:6

The LORD is gracious and compassionate, slow to anger and rich in *love*. Psalm 145:8

For great is his *love* toward us, and the faithfulness of the LORD endures forever. Praise the LORD.
Psalm 117:2

When I said, "My foot is slipping," your unfailing *love*, LORD, supported me.

Psalm 94:18

Daughters of Jerusalem, I charge you: Do not arouse or awaken *love* until it so desires. Song of Songs 8:4

Better a small serving of vegetables with *love* than a fattened calf with hatred.

Proverbs 15:17

Keep your lives free from the *love* of money and be content with what you have, because God has said, "Never will I leave you; never will I forsake you."
Hebrews 13:5

For the LORD is good and his *love* endures forever; his faithfulness continues through all generations.

Psalm 100:5

Do not forsake wisdom, and she will protect you; *love* her, and she will watch over you.

Proverbs 4:6

Let them give thanks to the LORD for his *unfailing love* and his wonderful deeds for mankind,

Psalm 107:15

the LORD delights in those who fear him, who put their hope in his *unfailing love*.

Psalm 147:11

Because of the LORD's great *love* we are not consumed, for his compassions never fail. Though he brings grief, he will show compassion, so great is his *unfailing love*.

Lamentations 3:22, 32

This is my command: *Love* each other.

I *love* those who *love* me, and those who seek me find me.

Proverbs 8:17

Whoever would foster *love* covers over an offense, but whoever repeats the matter separates close friends. 💙

Proverbs 17:9

Whoever loves his brother abides in the light, and in him there is no cause for stumbling.
1 John 2:10

and walk in the way of love, just as Christ loved us and gave himself up for us as a fragrant offering and sacrifice to God."
Ephesians 5:2

But I tell you, *love* your enemies and pray for those who persecute you, If you *love* those who *love* you, what reward will you get? *Are not even the tax collectors doing that?*

Matthew 5:44,46

"As the Father has loved me, so have I loved you. Now remain in my love. If you keep my commands, you will remain in my *love*, just as I have kept my Father's commands and remain in his *love*.

John 15:9-10

The LORD appeared to us in the past, saying: "I have loved you with an everlasting *love*; I have drawn you with unfailing kindness.

Jeremiah 31:3

"But God demonstrates his own *love* for us in this: While we were still sinners, Christ died for us."

Romans 5:8

"For God so *loved* the world that he gave his one and only Son, that whoever believes in him shall not perish but have eternal life."

John 3:16

www.ingramcontent.com/pod-product-compliance
Lightning Source LLC
Chambersburg PA
CBHW062006090426
42811CB00005B/764